Text © 2008 by Susan Beal
Designs © 2008 by Susan Beal, except where
noted, p. 5, 9, 11, 19
Photographs © 2008 by Burcu Avsar and
Zach DeSart
Illustrations © 2008 by The Taunton Press, Inc.

The material was previously published in the
book *Bead Simple Essential Techniques for Making
Jewelry Just the Way You Want It*
(ISBN 978-1-56158-953-1)
First published in this format 2012

The Taunton Press
Inspiration for hands-on living®

The Taunton Press, Inc., 63 South Main Street,
PO Box 5506, Newtown, CT 06470-5506
e-mail: tp@taunton.com

Interior Design and Layout: Susan Fazekas
Illustrator: Alexis Hartman
Photographers: Burcu Avsar and Zach DeSart

The following manufacturers/names appearing in
Drop Earrings are trademarks: eBay®

Printed in the United States of America
10 9 8 7 6 5 4 3 2 1

NOTE: These symbols are used at the
start of each project:

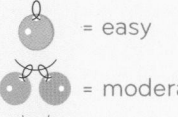

= easy

= moderate

= advanced

Table of Contents

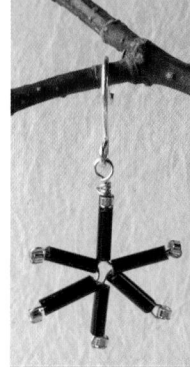

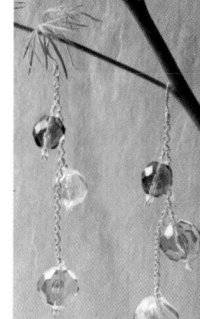

1

Earrings

Duo Earrings

This elegant pairing can be long and dramatic or charmingly compact.
Just choose beads that complement one another
and have fun with the basic design.

TECHNIQUES

- **Wrapped loops**
  All

- **Plain loops**
  All

- **Jump rings**
  Beachy Duo

- **Briolettes**
  Tangled Up
  in Blues

TIP Try an asymmetrical look (as in the Warm and Sparkly version) to embellish the basic concept. For one earring, add a wrapped loop at the base of bead A, then a small charm.

Warm and Sparkly Duo Earrings

These beautiful brown and gold Lucite beads swing low on chain, with a charming little locket mixed in for good measure.

Length: 4 inches

Warm and Sparkly Duo Earrings

YOU'LL NEED

- Pliers

- Thin chain
- 24-gauge wire
- Seed beads
- 2 pairs of beads (bead A is the faceted one and bead B is the round)
- One small charm
- Leverback earring wires

1. Cut two 3-inch pieces of chain and four 3-inch pieces of wire.

2. Form a plain loop at the end of one of the pieces of wire, and make a basic bead dangle by adding a seed bead, one of the two B beads, and another seed bead. Form the first half of a wrapped loop above it. Repeat with the second piece of wire.

3. Slip one of the bead dangles onto the end of a piece of chain and complete the wrap to join them. Repeat with the second dangle on the second piece of chain.

4. Form a plain loop at the end of the third piece of wire, and add a seed bead, one of the two A beads, and another seed bead. Form the first half of a wrapped loop above it.

5. Take the last piece of wire and form the first half of a wrapped loop on it. Slip the small charm onto the loop and finish the wrap. Now add a seed bead, the other A bead, and another seed bead, and form the first half of a wrapped loop above it.

6. Place each of the two bead-A dangles on the opposite ends of the chains from the bead-B dangles, finishing the wrap to join them.

7. Gently open one of the leverback rings and slip the first chain on, about ½ inch above the bead-A dangle. Close the leverback securely. Repeat with the second leverback and second piece of chain.

Tangled Up in Blues Earrings

These earrings spotlight an assortment of fun beads in the same color family. Here, two blue beads are suspended from one costume pearl on sterling.

Length: 2¾ inches

YOU'LL NEED

- Pliers

- 24-gauge wire

- Thin chain

- 2 of each of the following beads: small cube (A), round, and top-drilled teardrop (B)

- 2 round pearls

- Earring wires

1. Cut six 3-inch pieces of wire and two ⅝-inch pieces of chain. Form a plain loop at the bottom of two of the pieces of wire and add a cube to each one. Complete a wrapped loop above each piece to make basic bead dangles and set them aside.

2. Using two more pieces of wire, create a double-wrapped loop at the top of each teardrop, but don't close the top half yet. Make sure the top circle faces front on each one. Slip each of the teardrop dangles onto one end of each of the two pieces of chain and complete the wraps to join them.

3. Take the last two pieces of wire and form a wrapped loop at one end on each of them. Add a round pearl to each one, and form the first half of a wrapped loop above them.

4. Take one round dangle and slip the end link of the chain and the loop above the cube dangle into the open loop. Complete the wrap to join them. Repeat with the other three pieces so you have two identical earrings.

5. Open the earring wire loops, and slip the top loops of the rounds onto each one. Close the loops to join them.

Beachy Duo Earrings

This summery design by craft writer Nancy Flynn mixes pearls and nautical charms.

Length: 2 inches

TIP Try contrasting the weights of chain you use—many stores offer silver chain that looks like a miniature version of the chains used on ship anchors, which adds to the nautical look.

Beachy Duo Earrings

YOU'LL NEED

- Pliers
- 4 inches fine chain
- 2 inches of slightly thicker chain
- Two 1cm-diameter coin pearls
- 8 fine-gauge silver headpins
- Four 6mm blue faceted glass beads
- Two 6mm clear faceted glass beads
- Four 4mm-diameter jump rings
- 2 small charms
- Leverback earring wires

1. Cut two 2-inch pieces of fine chain and two 1-inch pieces of thicker chain.

2. Thread one pearl on a headpin, and form the first half of a wrapped loop at the top of the pearl. String the half loop through the last link in one 2-inch fine chain piece, and complete the wrapped loop so the pearl hangs at the end of the chain.

3. Thread a blue bead on a second headpin, and form the first half of a wrapped loop. String the half loop two links above the pearl and complete the wrapped loop. Repeat twice, skipping two links above the blue bead to add a clear one, and finishing two links above that with another blue bead.

4. Repeat steps 2 and 3 with the second 2-inch chain piece, pearl, and glass beads.

5. Gently open a jump ring with pliers and use it to join one charm loop and the final link of a 1-inch chain piece. Attach a second jump ring to the other free end of the chain piece. Repeat with the second 1-inch chain piece, charm, and jump rings.

6. Gently open one of the leverback rings and slip on the open end of one 2-inch chain and the jump ring at the non-charm end of one 1-inch piece. Close the leverback securely. Repeat with the second leverback and second set of chains.

Trio Earrings

Trio earrings use three drops in a flurry of different lengths to create a similar but more ornate design. Mix and match size, shape, and material for an eye-catching, swingy piece.

TECHNIQUES

- **Wrapped loops**
  Color Pop
  Glossy Carnelian

- **Jump rings**
  Lacy

- **Hand sewing**
  Lacy

TIP Use beads from your pendant or necklace designs to make complementary earrings.

Glossy Carnelian Trio Earrings

These elegant earrings match the Glossy Carnelian Tiered Necklace in Taunton's companion booklet, Bead Necklaces. (See page 32 for details.)

Length: 4 inches

YOU'LL NEED

- Pliers

- Thin chain

- 24-gauge sterling wire
- Seed beads
- Two ¾-inch oval beads
- Four 8mm faceted beads
- Leverback earring wires

Glossy Carnelian Trio Earrings

1. Cut two pieces of chain in each length: ½ inch, 1¼ inches, and 2 inches long, for a total of six pieces.

2. Cut two 3-inch pieces and four 2-inch pieces of wire. Form a plain loop at the end of each piece of wire.

3. On the two 3-inch wires, add a seed bead, a ¾-inch oval, and another seed bead. On the four 2-inch wires, add a seed bead, an 8mm bead, and another seed bead. Form the first half of a wrapped loop above each of the six dangles.

4. Join two of the 8mm dangles to the ends of the ½-inch length of chain, completing the wraps. Repeat with the other two 8mm dangles and the 1¼-inch pieces of chain.

5. Join the oval dangles to the 2-inch pieces of chain and complete the wraps.

6. Open one of the leverback rings and slip on one of each length of chain, longest first, then medium, then shortest. Close the leverback.

7. Repeat step 6 to finish the second earring.

Color Pop Trio Earrings

Lime green mother-of-pearl beads and tiny glass rounds are a fun combination.

Length: 2½ inches

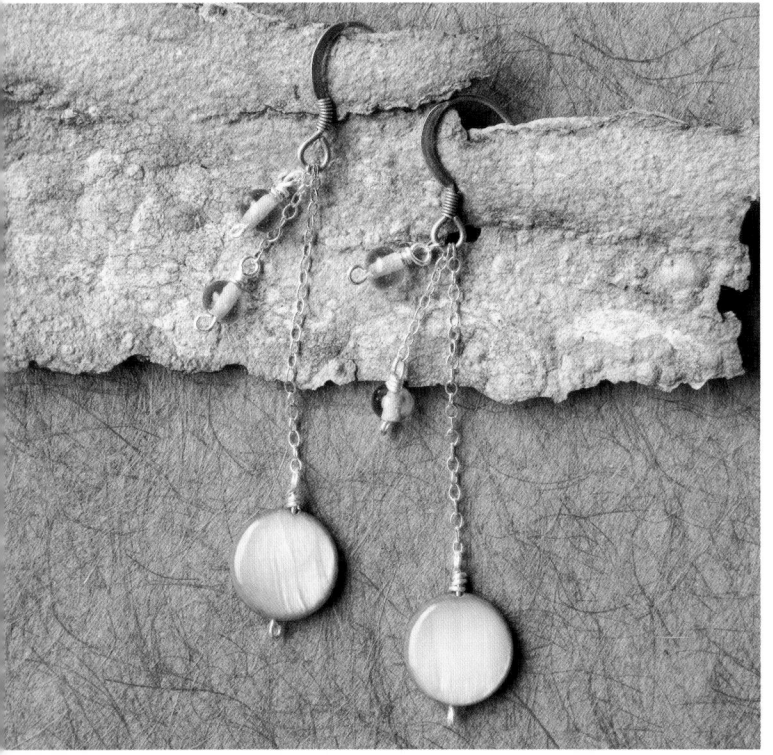

YOU'LL NEED

- Pliers
- 24-gauge wire
- Two 8mm mother-of-pearl lime green flat rounds
- 4 tiny lime green glass rounds
- Thin chain
- 2 earring wires

1. Cut six pieces of wire: two 2 inches long and four 1½ inches long. Form a plain loop at the end of each one.

2. Place the 8mm flat rounds on the longer wire pieces and the smaller beads on the shorter pieces. Form a wrapped loop above each one but don't close any of them yet.

3. Cut six pieces of chain: two that are only two links long, two that are ½ inch long, and two that are 1 inch long. Add one of the small beads to each of the shorter pieces of chain and complete the wrapped loops. Now add the two 8mm beads to the two 1-inch pieces of chain and complete the loops.

4. Open one of the earring wires and slip one of each chain length onto its loop, shortest to longest from front to back.

5. Repeat with the second earring wire and close both of them securely.

Lacy Trio Earrings

Designed by Kayte Terry, these delicate earrings include lace. Kayte is the author of Paper Made! *and* Appliqué Your Way. *She blogs at www.Thisisloveforever.com.*

Length: 3 inches

TIP Kayte suggests "Save lace scraps from sewing projects for making these earrings. I've scored lots of these floral decal beads on eBay®, but you can find new ones at jewelry-supply stores, too."

YOU'LL NEED
- Fabric scissors
- Paintbrush
- Fabric stiffener
- Waxed paper
- Sewing needle and thread
- Pliers and wire cutters

- Small pieces of lace
- Assorted sequins and small pearls
- Thin gold chain
- Four 3mm jump rings
- 4 teardrop-shaped floral decal beads (or any other drop beads)
- Two 5mm jump rings
- 4 small white beads
- 2 headpins
- Earring wires

1. Cut two shapes out of lace using small fabric scissors.

2. Brush fabric stiffener onto the lace pieces, and lay them out on waxed paper to dry. Let the lace completely dry, then repeat on the other side.

3. Once the lace pieces are dry, sew on sequins and small pearls using a needle and thread. Sew them in the same place on both sides so the stitches won't be seen. Make a small knot at the end of each and hide it behind a bead or pearl.

4. Cut two pieces of chain in each length: 2 inches, 1 inch, and ½ inch.

5. Attach the lace pieces to the 2-inch-long chains with a 3mm jump ring. Attach two teardrop-shaped beads to each of the 1-inch-long chains with a 5mm jump ring.

6. Add two small beads each to the two headpins. Form a small, plain loop and cut the excess wire with wire cutters, but do not close the loop. Slip the ½-inch length of chain onto each of the loops and close the wire.

7. Open a 3mm jump ring and slide on one earring wire, followed by one of each length of chain, longest first, then medium, then shortest. Close the jump ring.

8. Repeat step 7 to finish the second earring.

Modern Drop Earrings

These drop earrings are gorgeously simple and easy to wear,
either with coordinating pendant designs or on their own. Clean lines and
organic materials like wood and semiprecious stones lend a stylish sensibility.

TECHNIQUES

- **Wrapped loops**
  Wood
  Amber

- **Plain loops**
  Scrolled Wood
  Amber

- **Briolette/top wrapping**
  Wood

TIP For a different look, replace the wood with amber and make a basic dangle with the two large beads, leaving the top loop open. Slip each dangle onto a 1.5 inch piece of circle chain and complete the wrap. Then add earring wires, as shown at right.

Sleek Drop Earrings x3

These classic drop earrings can be made 3 ways: plain and simple, etched with a design, or dressed up with a semi-precious stone drop instead of wood.

Length: 4 inches

YOU'LL NEED

- Pliers
- Thin chain
- 24-gauge wire
- 2 elongated wood drops (horizontally drilled)
- 4 small semiprecious round beads
- Earring wires

1. Cut six ⅜-inch-long pieces of chain, two 4-inch pieces of wire, and four 3-inch pieces of wire. Wrap each wood drop briolette-style with a 4-inch piece, completing the coil above the bead. Then create the first half of a wrapped loop above the coil.

2. Slip the loop above one wood drop into the last link of a piece of chain, and complete the loop.

3. Using the first 3-inch piece of wire, form the first half of a wrapped loop and slip it onto the last link of one of the ⅜-inch pieces of chain, completing the wrap.

4. Place a small round bead on the wire and form the first half of a wrapped loop above it. Slip it onto the last link of the second ⅜-inch piece of chain, and complete the wrap.

5. Repeat steps 3 and 4 to create a second wrapped bead, linking the second and third pieces of chain.

6. Next, slip the earring wire loop into the last link at one end of the beaded chain you created.

7. Repeat the steps to complete the second earring.

8. For a different look, choose a lighter wood and etch or draw a design. Use jump rings and small wood beads to create the dangles. (Scrolled Wood Drop Earrings designed by Caitlin Troutman.)

Amber Bits Multi-Drop Earrings

Three amber bits swing on sterling wire.

Length: 2 inches

YOU'LL NEED

- Pliers
- Six 24-gauge headpins
- 6 small vertically drilled oval beads (like these asymmetrical amber pieces)
- Earring wires with forward-facing rings

1. Cut two of the headpins to ⅞ inch (S), two to 1¼ inches (M), and two to 1¾ inches (L) long.

2. Slip one bead onto each headpin, and form a flat-front plain loop at the top of each. Open your earring wire loops.

3. Take one headpin of each length and slip them onto an earring wire in this order (left to right): S, L, M. Close the earring wire.

4. Repeat step 3 to make the second earring.

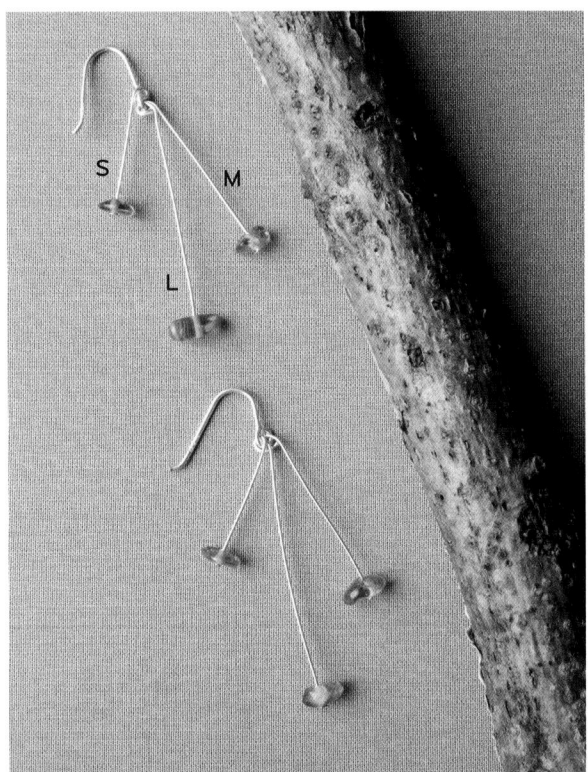

Black Starburst Earrings

An elegant version of the basic starburst with black glass bugle beads and silver delicas.

Length: 1¼ inches

YOU'LL NEED

- Pliers
- 28-gauge wire
- 12 delicas (or other tiny seed bead)
- Twelve ⅜-inch black bugle beads
- Earring wires

1. Cut an 18-inch piece of wire, and slip a single delica on it, sliding it down to the middle of the wire. Think of the half of the wire extending off to the left as side A and the half extending off to the right as side B.

2. Add a bugle bead to side A, slipping it all the way down to the delica. Thread the end of side B through the bugle bead, away from the delica, and gently pull it taut so that both ends of the wire extend out the same side of the bead, with the delica firmly anchored at the other end. This is your first "spike" of the asterisk and will be the bottom of the finished piece.

Black Starburst Earrings

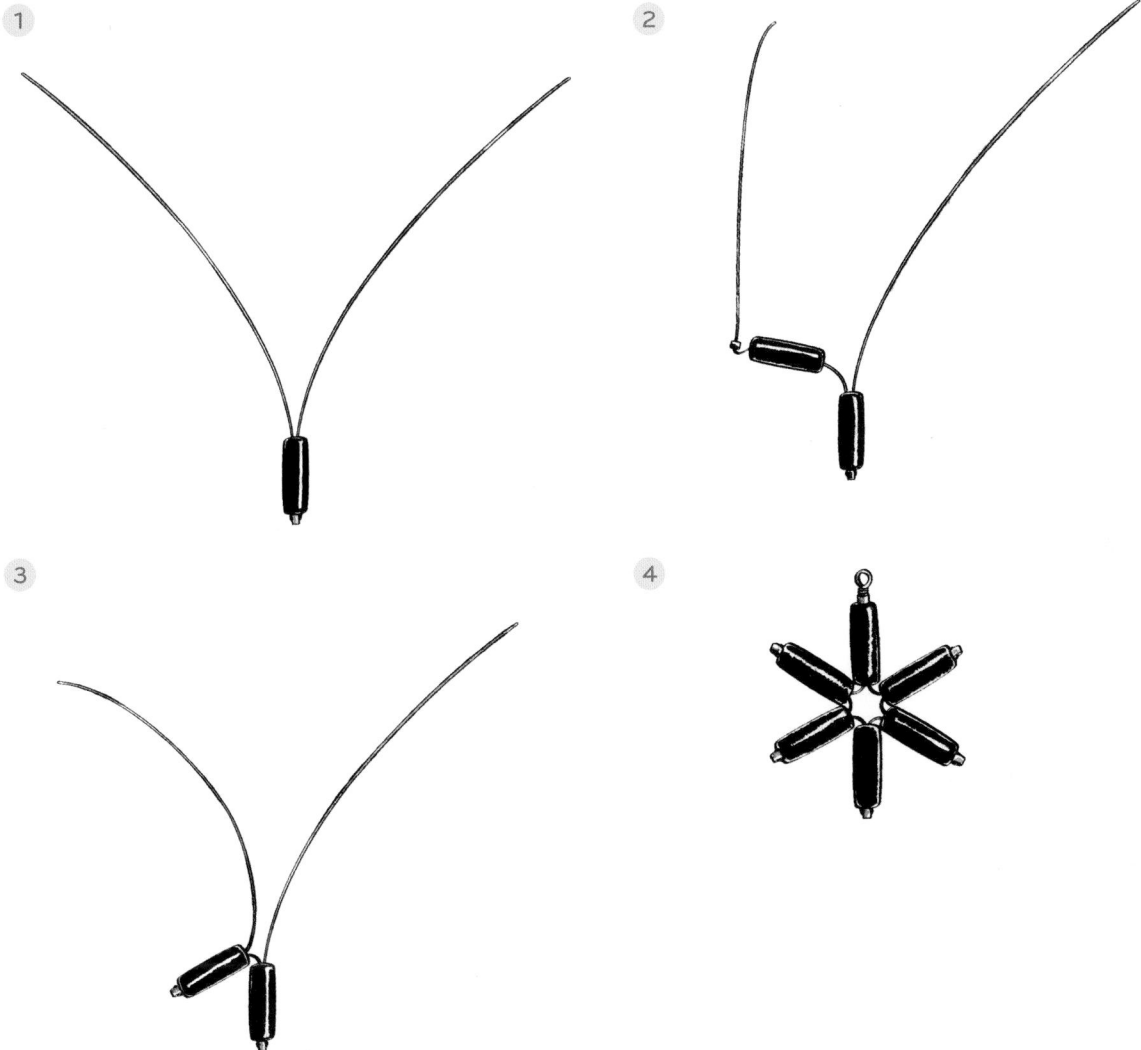

3. Next, you'll build one side of the starburst using side A only. Add a bugle bead and then a delica. Thread the tail of side A back through the bugle bead and gently pull it tight.

4. Repeat step 3 to create a third spike.

5. Now you'll make two spikes on the other side using side B—just repeat steps 3 and 4 to build them.

6. Sides A and B are now ready to unite to create the top spike. Slip a bugle bead onto side A and add a delica. Slip side B through the two beads in the same way so the two wire tails extend above the beads. Gently pull them taut.

7. Gently adjust the spikes so they radiate out evenly from the center. When you like the arrangement, form a wrapped loop using both strands of wire at the top of the piece.

8. Repeat steps 1–7 to create a second starburst piece.

9. Open the earring wire loops, and slip one starburst on each one. Close them securely.

Circle Deluxe Earrings

This earring concept ranges from elaborate embellished double circles to simpler mod singles—but one thing they all have in common is eye-catching style.

TECHNIQUES

- **Jump rings**
  Sparkling Star
  Wood

- **Briolette/top style**
  Wood

- **Wire looping**
  Sparkling Star

- **Plain loops**
  Red Rounds

- **Double-wrapped loops**
  Wood

Sparkling Star Circle Deluxe Earrings

These starry circle-within-a-circle earrings are just the thing to wear whenever you want a little sparkle and shine.

Length: 3 inches

YOU'LL NEED

- Pliers
- 24-gauge wire
- 12 small faceted beads
- Two star charms
- Six 3mm jump rings
- Two 1¼-inch circle drops
- Two 2-inch circle drops
- A short piece of thin chain
- Earring wires

1. You'll start by creating the embellished outer circle. Cut two 12-inch pieces of 24-gauge wire and begin wrapping the first circle, with the tail to the back, at the top of one circle. Wrap it closely until you've covered about a ½ inch of the hoop, then slip one faceted bead onto your wire tail. Wrap it securely so it sits on the front side of the circle, and continue your wraps the same way.

2. Add the other five beads in the same way, ½ inch apart—if the circle were a clock face, you'd place the beads at the 1, 3, 5, 7, 9, and 11 o'clock spots. Wrap the wire securely to end the embellishment when you reach the other side of the top.

3. Embellish the second outer circle the same way.

4. Suspend one star charm inside each of the two smaller circles using jump rings.

5. Connect one of the smaller circle drops inside one of the larger ones using a jump ring. Repeat with the other two circles.

6. Cut two very short lengths of the chain, making sure that you use an odd number of links so the earring will hang correctly—I used three links for each of mine, which were about ⅛ inch long. Connect one piece of chain above each of the circles using jump rings.

7. Open the earring wires, and slip the top loop of each chain into each one, making sure the earrings are facing front. Close them securely.

Red Rounds Circle Deluxe Earrings

This version is another double circle, capturing trios of red beads.

Length: 1¾ inches

Red Rounds Circle Deluxe Earrings

YOU'LL NEED

- Pliers
- 22-gauge wire
- 12 oversize seed beads
- Two 5mm soldered rings
- Earring wires

1. Cut two pieces of wire that are 1½ inches long and two pieces 3 inches long. Form a plain loop at the end of each piece.

2. String three beads on each piece of wire, and form a plain loop at the opposite end of each piece.

3. Take one of the shorter pieces and open both plain loops. Gently curve it into a circle shape.

The wire will resist, but just hold it in place for a moment.

4. Slip the open loops onto the first soldered ring, then close them.

5. Repeat steps 3 and 4 to attach the second "circle" to the second soldered ring.

6. Next, take one of the longer pieces and curve it into a circle shape as in step 3. Open both plain loops and slip them onto the first ring, outside the smaller circle. Close them to secure the piece.

7. Repeat step 6 to form and add the second larger circle to the second piece.

8. Open the earring wires and slip the soldered rings onto them. Close them securely.

Wood Circle Deluxe Earrings

Wood rounds lend a sweet, natural look.

Length: 1⅝ inches

YOU'LL NEED

- Pliers
- 24-gauge wire
- 2 mod circles (mine were drilled front to back)
- Earring wires

1. Cut two 3-inch pieces of wire, and form a double-wrapped loop above each mod circle.

2. Open the earring wires, and slip a mod circle drop into each one. Close the wire loops securely.

Low and Swingy Earrings

These earrings are long, low, and deliberately slightly different
from one another. Randomly adorn the lengths of chain with cool beads
or charms to create a look that's "match-y"—but unexpected.

TECHNIQUES

- **Plain loops**
  Caribbean

- **Wrapped loops**
  All

- **Briolette/top wrapping**
  Leaves

Caribbean Low and Swingy Earrings

These island-inspired earrings in greens and blues are always fun to wear.

Length: 4 inches

YOU'LL NEED

- Pliers
- Medium-size chain
- 24-gauge wire
- Clear seed beads
- 6 assorted beads in the same color family
- Earring wires

Caribbean Low and Swingy Earrings

1. Cut two 2½-inch pieces of chain and six 2-inch pieces of wire.

2. Form a plain loop at the end of each piece of wire. Place a seed bead, a bead, and another seed bead on each one. Form the first half of a wrapped loop above each one.

3. Randomly place three of the beads along the first piece of chain until you like the configuration. Attach each one to a link of chain, completing the wrap on each one.

4. Repeat step 3 with the other three beads and the second piece of chain.

5. Open both earring wires and slip the first link of one piece of chain into each one. Close them securely.

Leaves Low and Swingy Earrings

Long and lovely, these earrings feature leaves in an asymmetrical pattern.

Length: up to 6 inches (adjustable)

YOU'LL NEED
- Pliers
- Thin chain
- 24-gauge wire
- 2 large (1-inch) leaf charms
- 3 small (⅝-inch) leaf charms
- Chain earring wires
- Jump rings

1. Cut two 3-inch pieces of chain and five 2-inch pieces of wire.

2. Create a wrapped loop briolette-style on each of the large leaf charms. Form the first half of a wrapped loop above the coil on one and slip it onto the last link of chain, completing the wrap. Repeat to join the second leaf to the second piece of chain.

3. Next, form a wrapped loop briolette-style above each of the three small leaf charms. Form the first half of a wrapped loop above each one.

4. Lay one piece of chain out flat and attach a small leaf charm to a link 1 inch above the large leaf charm, completing the wrap to join them. Set this piece aside.

5. Lay out the other piece of chain and measure ½ inch above the large leaf. Attach a small leaf charm there, completing the wrap to join them. Now measure 1 inch above that charm and add the last leaf there, completing that wrap to join them.

6. Attach each chain to an earring wire using a jump ring.

Pop Organic Low and Swingy Earrings

Designed by style maven Tricia Royal, these earrings mix wood with colorful accents. (See more of Tricia's work at bitsandbobbins.com.)

Length: 4½ inches

> **TIP** Try to find beads of different sizes to make these earrings: two large ones and a selection of small and medium-size beads in varying colors and textures. Pick out beads from your stash, and play around until you find a color combination that pleases your eye and your own personal taste.

YOU'LL NEED

- Pliers
- 2 large beads (18–20mm)
- 20-gauge gold wire
- Approximately 20 beads of various colors/sizes/shapes/textures (2–12mm or so)
- Ten to fourteen 2-inch headpins
- 3mm jump rings
- Two 1½-inch pieces of oversize gold chain (Tricia pilfered hers from a vintage necklace)

1. Make a basic dangle with the two large beads—you can add a small bead above and below the large ones if you like.

2. With the remaining beads and headpins, create basic dangles of various lengths. Use two or three beads on some, one or two on others.

3. Divide the dangles up between each of the earrings. Each earring should have one dangle with the large bead and five or six smaller dangles. Play around freely, but try to put approximately the same beads and colors on each of the earrings somewhere so they feel varied but are clearly a pair. Open one jump ring for each dangle.

4. Attach the dangles to the oversize chain with the jump rings. Place most of the dangles on the lowest link of the chain, but for variation and asymmetry, you can add some higher on the earring (especially smaller ones).

5. Open the last two jump rings and use them to connect the earring wires to the earrings you've created.

Techniques

Here are the techniques you'll use to create every design in this booklet—and more! You may need to practice some of them a few times before trying them out on a project, but they get much easier with a little trial and error. If you need help, there are short videos of many of these on beadsimple.com for reference, too.

Bead Stringing

Bead stringing is the most basic way to construct a piece of jewelry like a necklace or bracelet—just thread a needle or pick up a piece of flexible wire, secure the end, and add beads one after another. Depending on what you're using materials-wise and your own taste, there are several ways to construct your piece of jewelry.

Needle beading

1. Before you begin, you may want to add a bead tip (see facing page) to add your clasp or end component.

2. Thread a needle with your thinner material (like elastic, silk cord, or nylon thread), and tie a knot or cover the end with a doubled piece of tape.

3. Add your beads one (or more) at a time, and continue beading until you reach the desired length.

4. Finish with a bead tip or durable knotting (if no clasp is required).

Needle Beading

Finishing with Bead Tips

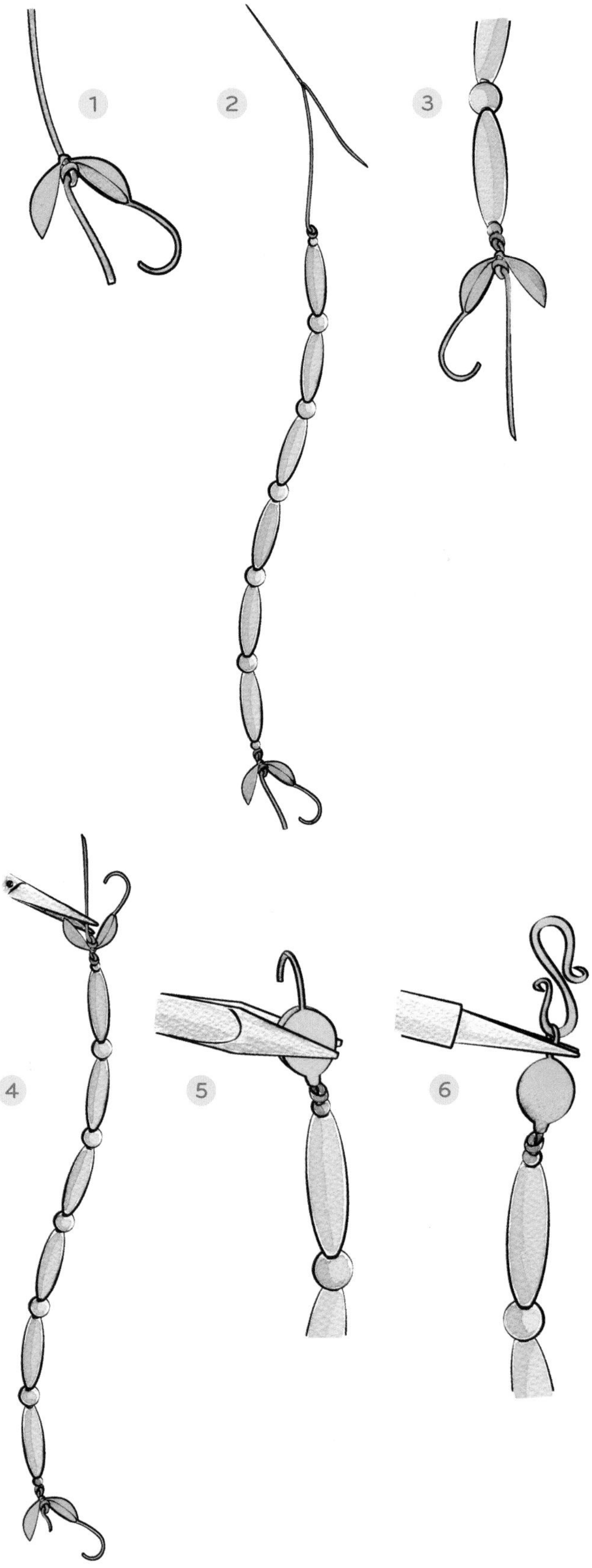

Finishing with bead tips

Bead tips cover a knot at each end of the cord securely, and the curved hook attaches to a finding. See complete instructions for knotting on p. 27.

1. Tie a knot near the beginning of your cord and slip one bead tip onto it, with the two cupping halves facing and enveloping the knot (as shown). Knot again directly above the bead tip to keep it in place.

2. String or knot your beads as you go until you're finished with your piece. Tie a knot at the end.

3. Add a bead tip with the halves facing outward, away from the beads and toward the needle. Using your knotting tweezers to pinpoint the spot, tie a knot inside the tip and pull it taut.

4. Add a drop of glue or Fray Check™ (I often use Fray Check, then glue), and snip the cord ends away just above each knot.

5. Using your flat-nose pliers, press the tips closed around the knots.

6. Using your round-nose pliers, curve the hook around a jump ring or clasp loop.

Flexible beading wire

This thin, durable wire is easy to bead with. Use good-quality materials—it's so worth it! I highly recommend Soft Flex wire, since inexpensive tiger-tail wire kinks and ages poorly.

1. Cut a piece of wire at least 4 to 6 inches longer than the finished length of the piece you're making. Add a doubled piece of clear tape near the end of your wire to hold your design as you string your pieces—it's easy to take off when you're ready to

4

5

6

Flexible Beading Wire

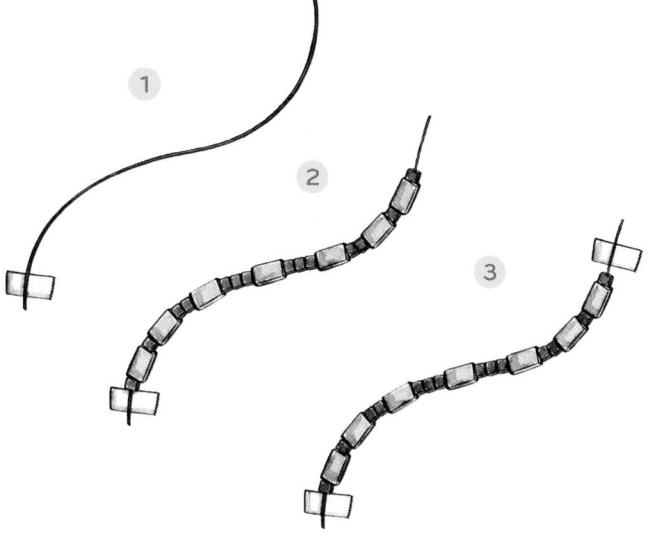

finish the ends but won't kink or untie itself as a knot often does.

2. Begin creating your design from one end, or construct the middle section and move outward—it's up to you. Beads will slip right onto your wire, so you don't need a needle. Just add them in the desired pattern, and remember, you can always tape the working end and switch back to the other side if you want to change your design—it's very flexible.

Crimp Beads

3. If you need to take a break or don't finish the project right away, just tape both ends of the wire to hold the pattern.

Crimp beads

Finish a Soft Flex or a ribbon piece with crimp beads—small metal cylinders that hold a doubled cord securely when you flatten or crimp them with pliers. They can also be used to hold a bead or piece in place on a single wire or cord or as a design element.

I recommend sterling or gold-filled cylinder-shaped crimp beads, which are easy to work with and finish smoothly. Base metal crimps can be rough at the edge, scratching your skin or cutting through the wire itself.

1. Finish stringing your piece. Place a single crimp bead on the end of the strand and add a clasp.

2. Slip the wire tail back through the crimp bead then through the next several beads.

3. Tug the wire so it's taut, with no gaps between beads or at the end.

4. Firmly crimp the bead closed with your flat-nose pliers.

5. Clip off the end of the wire close to the beads so the end tucks back in and won't scratch your skin.

TIP Use an oversize crimp bead if you are crimping more than two strands at a time, especially if it's a thicker Soft Flex wire.

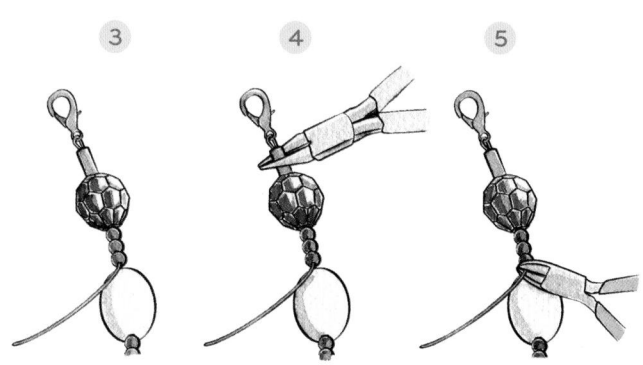

Crimp clasps

You'll attach all-in-one crimp/clasp pieces similarly. Just use your flat-nose pliers to securely flatten the metal crimp around the cord or ribbon. Crimp one side at a time if it's a flap style or the entire thing if it's a cylinder style. You may want to add a drop of glue to your cord before slipping it into the crimp clasp for extra hold.

Double crimp variation

You can also use special crimping pliers to make a double crimp with a tighter, cleaner finish.

1. Follow steps 1–3 for crimp beads, but instead of pressing the crimp bead flat in one motion as in step 4, position it inside the first notch of the crimping pliers (closest to the handles) and gently squeeze it, forming a curved U shape.

2. Place the curved crimp bead into the second notch (closer to the tips), rotate it 90 degrees, and squeeze again, tightening the U shape closed.

3. Finally, flatten the doubled crimp bead completely using the tip of the pliers.

Memory wire

Here's how to start—and finish—a necklace or bracelet made with memory wire.

1. Cut the memory wire round to the length you want it to be. Take a ball- or cube-shaped tip and use a small drop of glue to attach it to the end of the memory wire round on one side. Once it's completely dry, start adding beads.

2. When you finish your bead stringing, you should have a short "tail" of memory wire at the open end. Gripping the tail with your flat-nose pliers, gently shake the memory wire so the beads fall into place with no gaps between them. Place the tip on the end to see if there's any open space once it's on. If there

Memory Wire

Double Crimp

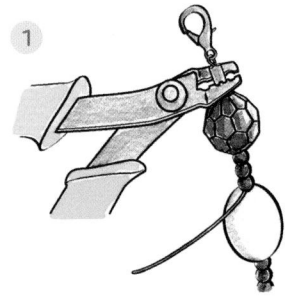
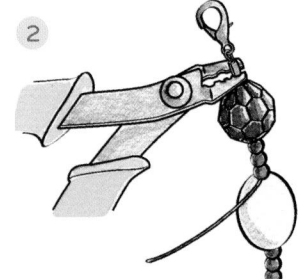

is, cut the tail more closely (you may need to take off a few beads, cut it, and put them back on) or add another seed bead.

3. Glue the last seed bead in place, then carefully glue the second tip onto the tail. Let it dry completely. Note: If you'd rather not glue your last bead, just glue the tip on the end of the wire.

Wirework

These basic techniques—forming plain loops and wrapped loops with your pliers—are easy steps that transform a simple piece of wire into a custom eyepin, earwire, chain link, or pendant. Plain and wrapped loops are the knit and purl stitches of jewelry making—they're invaluable for making just about anything, from simple drop earrings to elaborate wire masterpieces. Once you learn these basics, you'll be able to repair or alter jewelry and create and embellish new pieces.

In these diagrams, the flat-nose pliers are shown with blue handles, the round-nose pliers have red handles, and the wire cutters have black handles.

Plain loops

1. Cut a 4-inch piece of craft wire, then use your flat-nose pliers to bend it at a neat 90-degree angle about ¼ to ½ inch from the end. The longer the wire bend, the larger the loop.

2. Holding the longer part of the wire with your flat-nose pliers, grasp the end of the shorter wire bend with the tip of your round-nose pliers.

3. Twist your wrist so you begin to bring the very end of the wire around to meet the bend, forming a neat circle. You'll essentially be rolling the pliers toward you. It can be easier to do this in two steps, letting go of the wire about halfway through and then grasping it again with your pliers to finish bringing it around. You can adjust or finish the loop after you curve the wire so it's perfectly round.

4. The finished loop should look like a lollipop. If there is any excess wire extending beyond the circle, trim it with wire cutters and gently tweak it back into shape. If your loops are misshapen or crooked, just clip them off and start again.

Wrapped loops

1. Place a bead on the eyepin you've just created. Grasp the wire just above the bead with your round-nose pliers, and make another neat 90-degree angle bend above and over the tips, holding the wire tail with your flat-nose pliers.

2. Next, adjust the round-nose pliers so they are gripping on either side of the wire bend, above and below it. Use your flat-nose pliers to pull the wire tail over the end of the round-nose pliers and all the way around, creating a circle with an extra tail of wire still extending beyond it.

3. Use the flat-nose pliers to hold the circle while you grip the end of the wire tail with your round-nose pliers.

4. Wrap the wire tail around the space above the bead, working from top to bottom to create a neat

Plain Loops

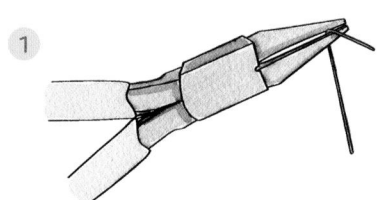
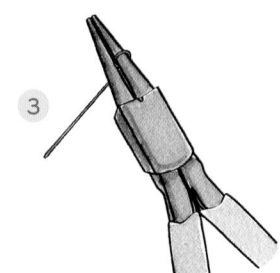

Wrapped Loops

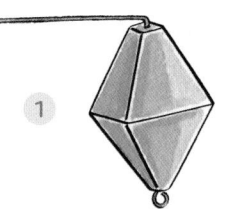
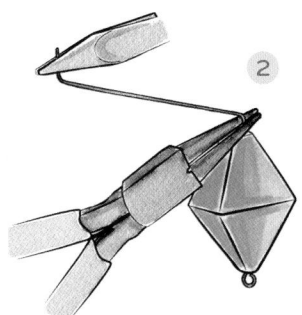
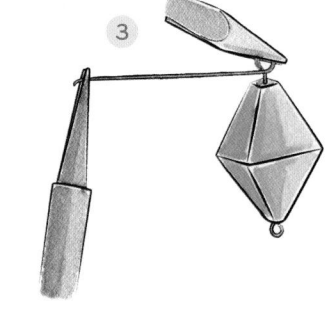
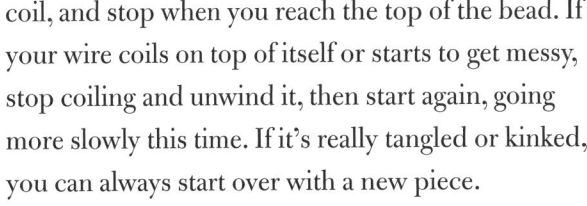

coil, and stop when you reach the top of the bead. If your wire coils on top of itself or starts to get messy, stop coiling and unwind it, then start again, going more slowly this time. If it's really tangled or kinked, you can always start over with a new piece.

5. Clip the end of the wire flush with the coil. Make sure the sharp edge isn't sticking out—if it does, use your flat-nose pliers to flatten and smooth it into the coil.

TIP Practice with inexpensive craft wire until your loops are nice and even.

TIP Plain loops work best with thick wire (such as 20 gauge), while the more secure wrapped loops are good for thinner wire (24 gauge).

BASIC DANGLE Creating a plain loop below a bead and a wrapped loop above it transforms the bead into a dangling charm as illustrated at right.

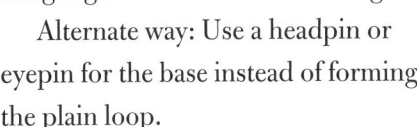

Alternate way: Use a headpin or eyepin for the base instead of forming the plain loop.

DOUBLE-LOOPED BEAD CONNECTOR Use this process to link a bead into a longer chain or design. Just cut a piece of wire and make a wrapped loop or a plain loop on each side, being sure to join the loops to the chain or design before you close them completely. As always, you'll use a wrapped loop

Flat-Front Plain Loop Variation

For this variation, the plain loop looks like a "P"—the curve of the loop is to the back of, say, a drop pendant. To do this, skip step 1 and grasp the end of the wire. Simply curve it into a loop. The wire will still look straight and smooth in front instead of obviously curved.

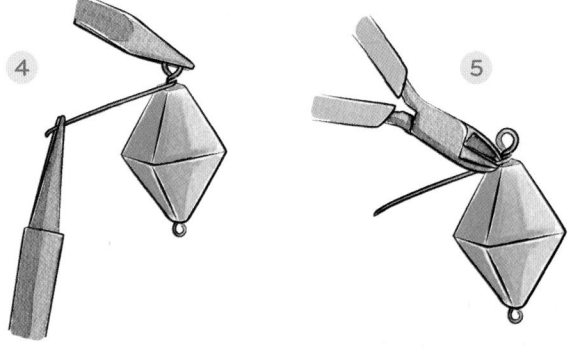
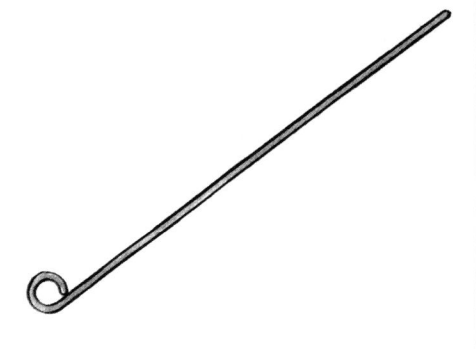

Double-Looped Connectors

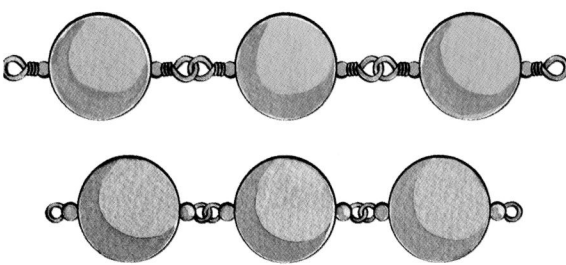

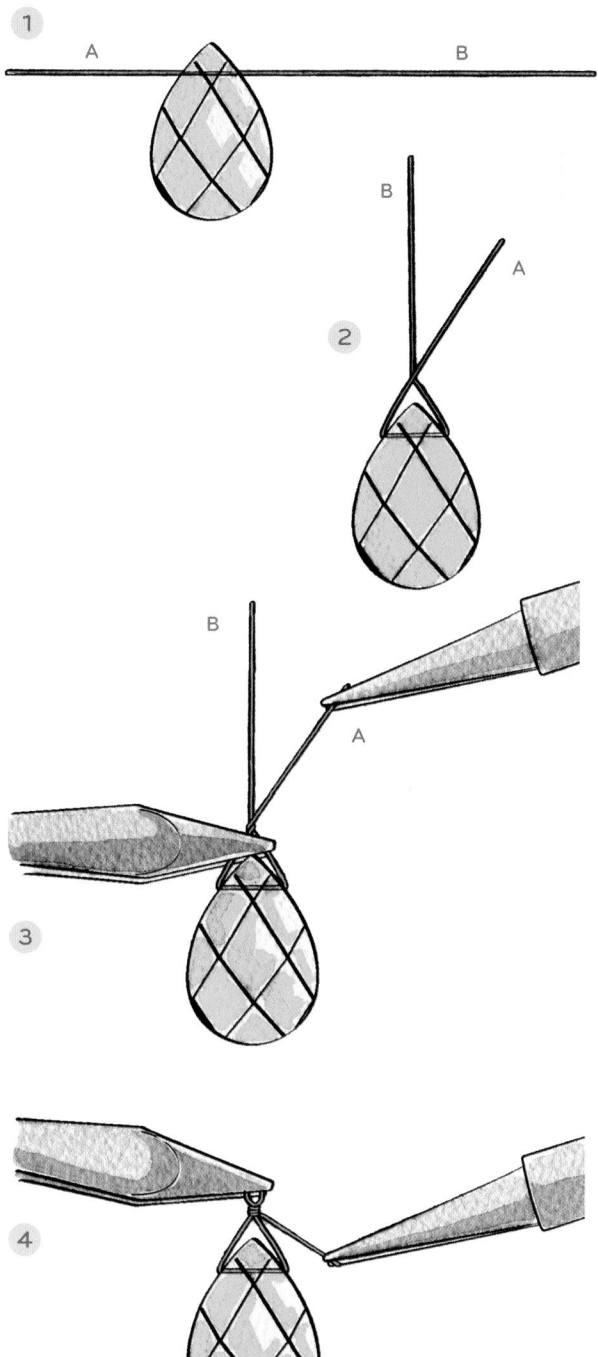

with a thinner-gauge wire (24 and up) and have the option of doing a plain loop with a heavier-gauge wire (20 and below). See the illustrations above.

Briolette wrapping

This technique is great for creating a handmade "hanger" for both horizontally drilled briolettes and pieces with a space in the middle. It's essentially a variation on the double-wrapped loop on the facing page.

1. Cut a 4-inch piece of wire and run it through a briolette, side to side, so one-third of the wire is on one side (A) and two-thirds on the other (B).

2. Fold one then the other wire up into a triangle, following the lines of the bead. The wires will look like an X.

3. Form a sharp angle in wire B so it extends straight above the bead.

4. Grip the wires below the X with flat-nose pliers, and wrap wire A in a coil around wire B. Stop after three coils and clip the wire.

5. Form a loop above the coil. Grip it with flat-nose pliers, using round-nose pliers to make a new coil starting at the top and moving downward.

6. Bring the wire tail around to the side of the coil where the tail from step 4 is and clip it closely. Use your flat-nose pliers to make sure the wire clipping is flush with the coil. This side will be the back of the finished piece, so the neat coiling shows continuously and the raw edges are hidden behind it.

Variation: Side-to-side briolette

Use this version to connect a single briolette to chain or cord on both sides, instead of making a drop to suspend from one strand. Cut a piece of wire and make a wrapped loop on one side, slipping it through the last link of a piece of chain before completing the wrap. Slip the briolette onto the wire and form a second wrapped loop on its other side, again adding it to a last link of chain before completing the wrap (see the drawing above).

You may also want to curve the loops upward.

Double-wrapped loop

This dual loop wraps around (or through) a charm or piece and the chain or cord to form a double connector or hanger. It's made the same way as a double-looped bead connector without the bead in the middle of the coils.

1. Cut a piece of wire and form a briolette-style hanger around or through the piece, front to back, leaving the top loop open after forming the first half. You'll wrap the coil using the back wire tail, going around the front piece.

2. Slip the open loop onto a chain or cord and complete the wrap, making sure the wire ends are tucked to the back of the coil so they don't show. As you wind the top wrap, the coil will stay neater if you bring the wire around on the opposite side from the first wrap.

Double-Wrapped Loop

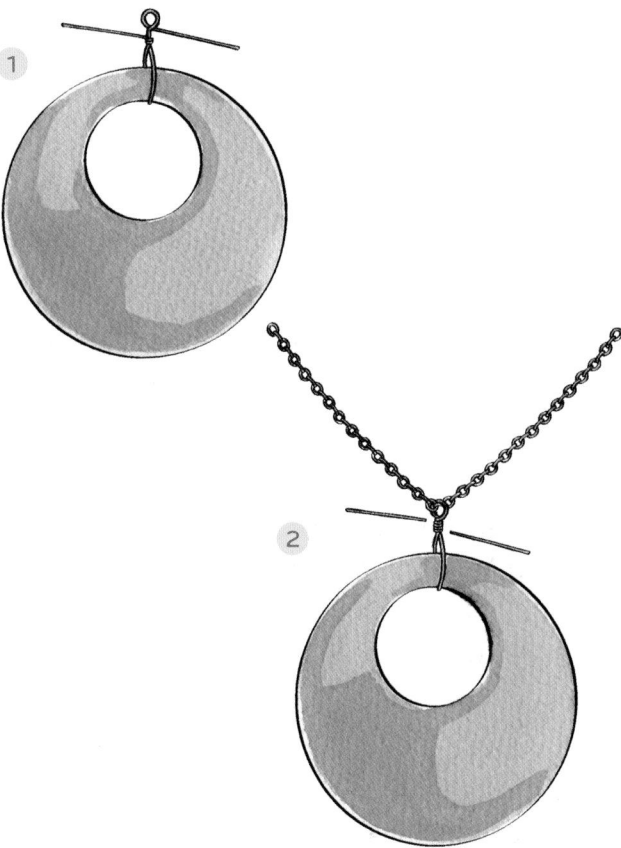

Wire looping

This technique is simple—just use wire to go through a bead once, back to front, bring it around to the back again, and slip it through a second time. It's great for securing small beads or holding larger ones.

1. Slip the bead onto the wire.

2. Bring the wire tail around and through the bead again.

3. Pull it tight so the wire hugs the bead.

Wire Looping

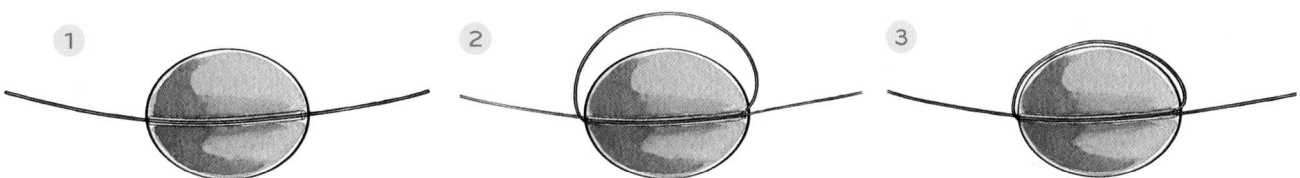

Jump rings

Use jump rings—small circles of wire with an opening—to attach clasps, suspend charms, or form a simple chain.

1. Open a jump ring by gripping the ring on each side with a pair of pliers. Separate the ring by tilting the right side toward you and the left side away from you—don't pull the ring open into a U shape.

2. Close the ring by reversing step 1. The ring should close neatly with no gap where the ends meet. If it doesn't meet neatly on the first try, gently tilt the two sides back and forth past the closed position a few times until the ring "clicks" shut. You can also make sure it's secure by squeezing it shut with the flat-nose pliers.

Jump Rings

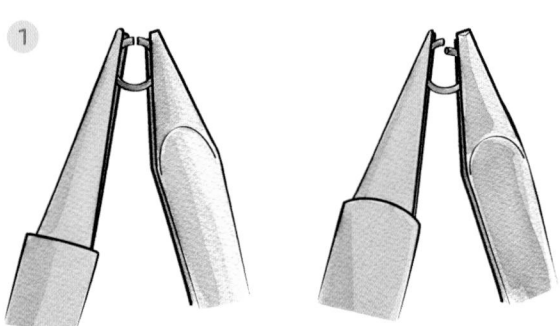

Basic Earring Wires

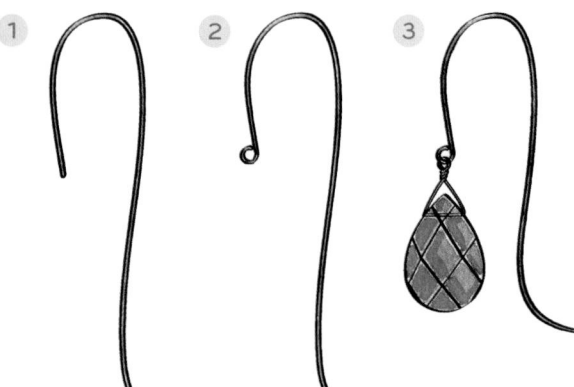

To attach a clasp to a chain, simply slip both the last link in the chain and the clasp (or its ring) onto the open jump ring in step 1. Close it to connect the two, as in step 2.

To attach a charm to a chain, choose the link you want to use and open a jump ring. Slip the charm or dangle onto the ring, then slip one end of the open ring through the link you've chosen. Close it securely.

To create a simple chain, just join a series of jump rings into a long row. Start with two: Open one, join it to the other, and close it. Add a third the same way, and so on until your chain is the desired length.

TIP If your jump ring becomes misshapen or dented from plier marks, just throw it away and start over with a new one.

Basic earring wires

1. Cut a 2½-inch piece of 22-gauge or 24-gauge wire, and form a large, round curve starting about ¾ inch in from the end. If the wire has a natural curve, follow it.

2. Next, create a small flat-front plain loop at the short end. This will be the loop of the earring wire.

3. Use your pliers to make a neat bend on the long end of the wire.

Eyepins

These are ultra-simple—just take a 1-inch to 4-inch piece of straight wire and form a plain loop at one end. That's it!

Clasps

Use your round-nose pliers to bend wire into clasp shapes, much like heavier-gauge versions of the earring wires. Pair these handmade clasps with soldered rings.

TIP Make different sizes of clasps by changing the length of the wire piece you work with. A 1½-inch wire will make an approximately ⅝-inch hook clasp, for example, and a 2-inch wire will make a ¾-inch S-clasp.

Hooks

1. Cut a 1½-inch to 2-inch piece of 16-gauge or 18-gauge wire. Following the natural curve of the wire, bend a curve into it just before the halfway point.

2. Form a small or medium-size plain loop at the shorter end, curving the wire out into a circle. This will be the hook end.

3. Now form a larger plain loop at the longer end. This loop will connect to the cord, chain, or jump ring.

4. Open the larger plain loop just as you would open a jump ring to attach it to your finding or chain.

S-clasp

1. Cut a 2-inch piece of 16-gauge or 18-gauge half-hard wire. Hold the wire about one-third of the way in on one side and make a curve in it, following the natural curve of the wire.

2. Make a second curve about one-third of the way in from the other side. Now you have a basic S shape (as shown).

3. Form a small plain loop at first one end of the S (the flat-front variation is fine, since the thicker wire will be harder to bend) and then the other.

4. Use your pliers to adjust the wire so one side is closed and the other is slightly open—this side will be the hook, and the closed side will be the connector.

Basic Bead Weaving

This pretty, but very basic, bead-weaving pattern is a nice embellishment for pendant necklaces and bracelets. Once you get the pattern down, it's surprisingly easy: You'll create a repetitive design with beads mirroring each other, and the two wires you weave with will pass through central beads that look like rungs on a ladder.

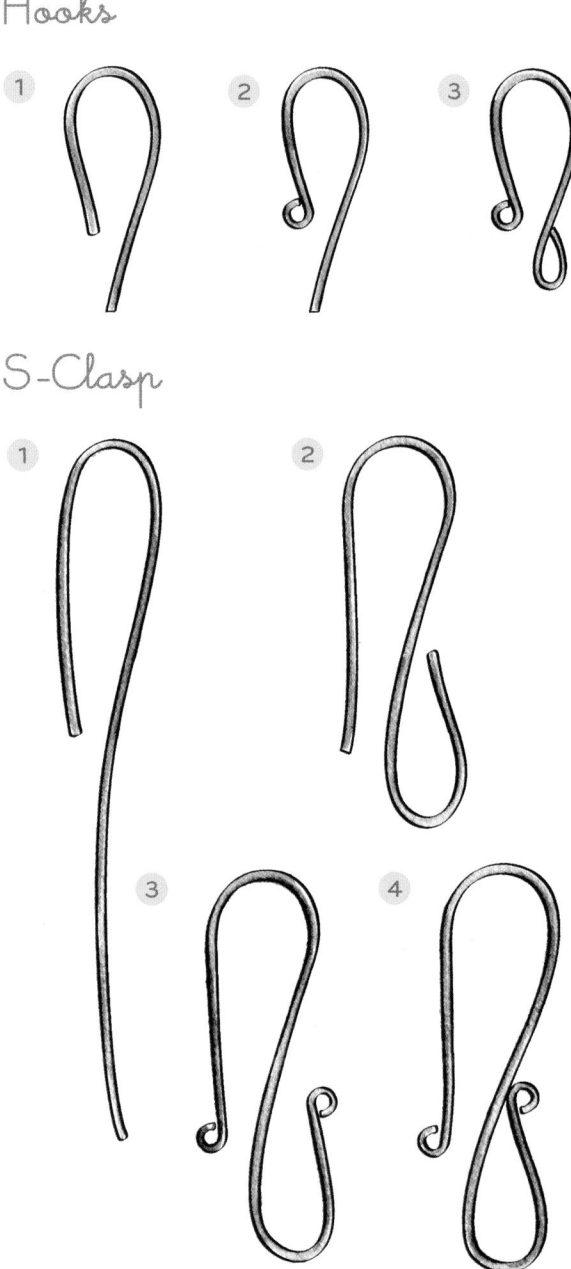

Hooks

S-Clasp

The main difference between the two projects is that the bracelets are symmetrical, while the necklaces have embellishments on the lower scallops. The necklace sits like a collar, so these projects have an adjustable chain back instead of a simple clasp. Always string this pattern on Soft Flex instead of stiffer wire. For very lightweight beads, you could also use silk or nylon cord with bead tips instead of crimp beads.

Basic Bead Weaving

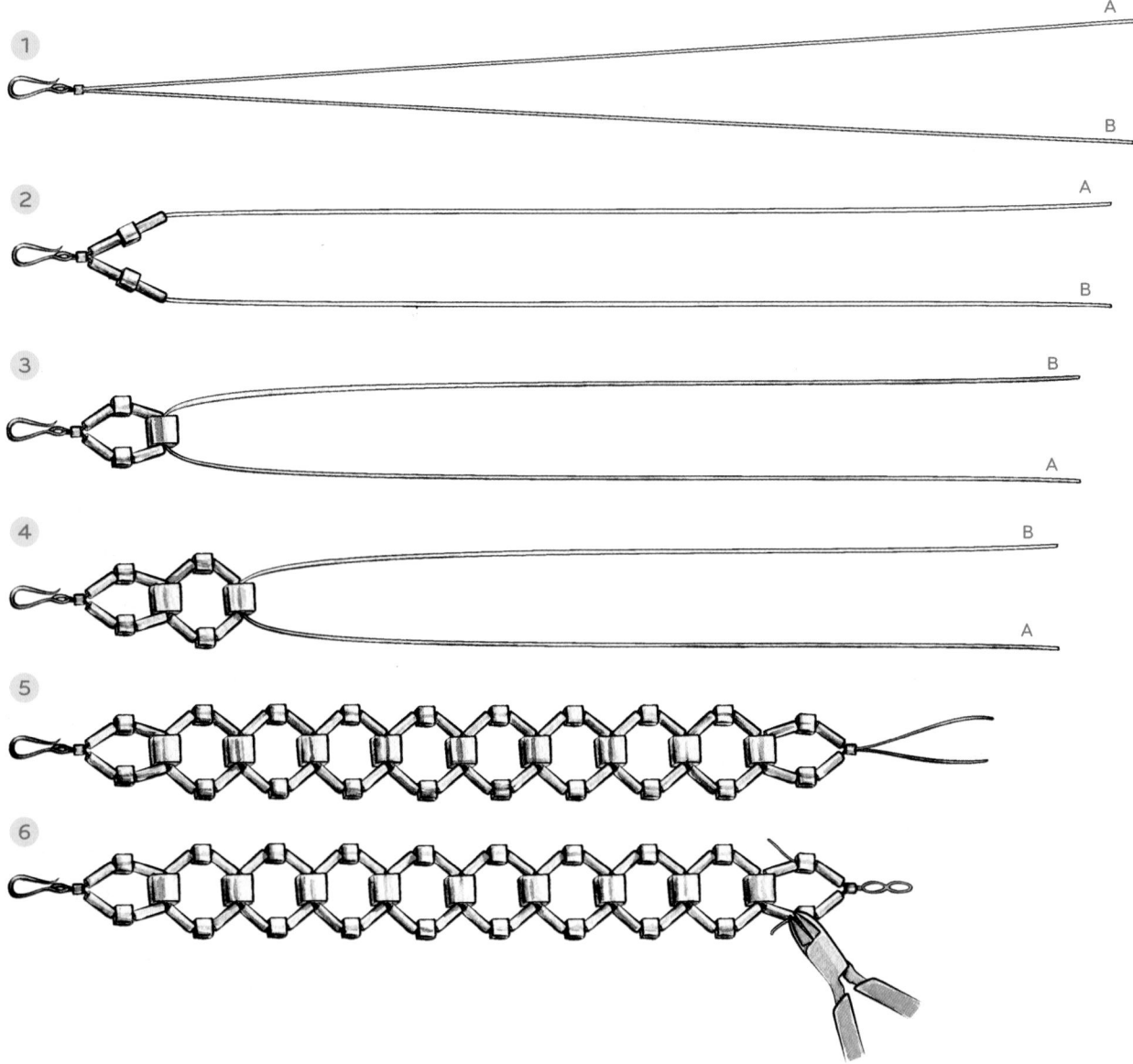

Bracelet/symmetrical style

1. Cut a 3-foot piece of beading wire and slip the clasp onto it. Add a crimp bead over both wire tails, and slip it all the way down the wire so it is just over the clasp or chain. Crimp it closed. You now have two 1½-foot wire tails extending out of the crimp bead to work with.

2. Think of the tail that is currently upper as A and the one that's currently lower as B. Begin your pattern by adding several beads to each strand to form the sides. For this sample pattern, string a bugle, a small bead, and another bugle on each strand.

3. Add a large central bead to A and then slip B through it, coming in the side that A exited. Pull the two tails tight so that the central bead is neatly holding the first few beads in place. A will now be lower and B upper since they have crossed inside the large bead.

4. Add a bugle, a small bead, and another bugle on each strand, then slip both wires through a large bead as you did in steps 2 and 3.

5. Continue until you have nine large beads strung. Add a bugle/small bead/bugle to each strand, then slip a crimp bead over both strands.

6. Slip the other half of your clasp onto both wires, and bring the wires back through the crimp bead. Slip one piece of wire through each of the beaded strands, and pull the tail through so the design is taut and symmetrical. Crimp the bead closed, then trim each of the wire tails.

Necklace/asymmetrical version

This method is very similar to the bracelet, with one major difference: The lower scallops have a drop or embellishment and the upper ones are simpler. There are two things to remember: First, since your wires will weave back and forth, the embellishments will not be strung on the same strand but alternate between A and B. Second, you'll need to balance your embellishments with beads above that have similar width so the pattern hangs well. Follow the same basic directions for making a bracelet style, but construct the necklace with chain on each side so it's adjustable in length, and use a drop ornament on all the odd-numbered segments and a small bead on the evens.

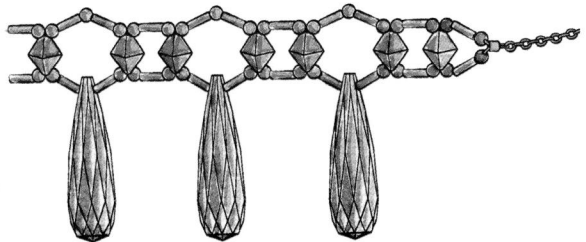

Knotting

Knotting between beads is easy—especially when you use narrow tweezers to pinpoint exactly where you want your knot to go. Use knotting to separate beads or to create spaces on a cord.

Knotting

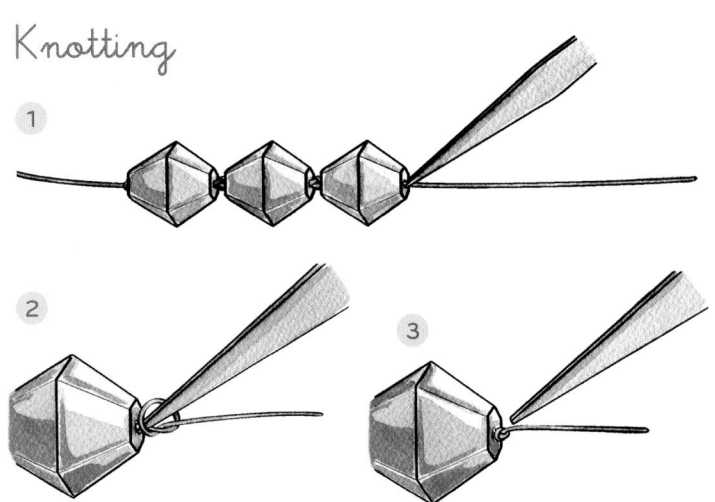

1. Choose where you want your knot to be, and grip that spot firmly with tweezers.

2. Bring your working cord around and over to tie a simple square knot over the tip of the tweezers.

3. Move the tweezers away just as you tighten the knot closed.

You can also use a row of knots to hold a larger piece.

Stitching

You can stitch beads, buttons, and charms onto fabric and ribbons as easily as threading a needle.

TIP If you are stitching your beads on with sewing thread (especially nice when you want to match your garment or ribbon's unusual color exactly), be sure to use 100 percent polyester thread instead of cotton, which is much less durable. For added resilience, cut your thread, run it through beeswax twice, and give it a quick iron (on the synthetic setting) to seal it. This process will strengthen your thread considerably. Match your bead weight to the fabric or ribbon you're embellishing—a thin material will sag with heavy beads attached, so use lighter-weight or smaller ones instead.

Look for these other THREADS Selects booklets at www.taunton.com and wherever crafts are sold.

Baby Beanies
Debby Ware

EAN: 9781621137634
8 ½ x 10 ⅞, 32 pages
Product# 078001
$9.95 U.S., $11.95 Can.

Fair Isle Flower Garden
Kathleen Taylor

EAN: 9781621137702
8 ½ x 10 ⅞, 32 pages
Product# 078008
$9.95 U.S., $11.95 Can.

Fair Isle Hats, Scarves, Mittens & Gloves
Kathleen Taylor

EAN: 9781621137719
8 ½ x 10 ⅞, 32 pages
Product# 078009
$9.95 U.S., $11.95 Can.

Lace Socks
Kathleen Taylor

EAN: 9781621137894
8 ½ x 10 ⅞, 32 pages
Product# 078012
$9.95 U.S., $11.95 Can.

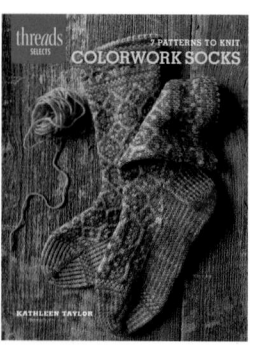

Colorwork Socks
Kathleen Taylor

EAN: 9781621137740
8 ½ x 10 ⅞, 32 pages
Product# 078011
$9.95 U.S., $11.95 Can.

DIY Bride Cakes & Sweets
Khris Cochran

EAN: 9781621137665
8 ½ x 10 ⅞, 32 pages
Product# 078004
$9.95 U.S., $11.95 Can.

DIY Bride Beautiful Bouquets
Khris Cochran

EAN: 9781621137672
8 ½ x 10 ⅞, 32 pages
Product# 078005
$9.95 U.S., $11.95 Can.

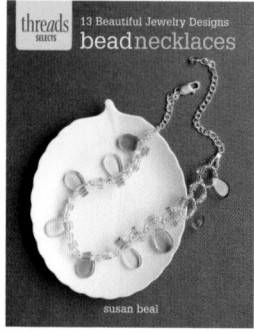

Bead Necklaces
Susan Beal

EAN: 9781621137641
8 ½ x 10 ⅞, 32 pages
Product# 078002
$9.95 U.S., $11.95 Can.

Drop Earrings
Susan Beal

EAN: 9781621137658
8 ½ x 10 ⅞, 32 pages
Product# 078003
$9.95 U.S., $11.95 Can.

Crochet Prayer Shawls
Janet Severi Bristow & Victoria A. Cole-Galo

EAN: 9781621137689
8 ½ x 10 ⅞, 32 pages
Product# 078006
$9.95 U.S., $11.95 Can.

Knitted Prayer Shawls
Janet Severi Bristow & Victoria A. Cole-Galo

EAN: 9781621137696
8 ½ x 10 ⅞, 32 pages
Product# 078007
$9.95 U.S., $11.95 Can.

Shawlettes
Jean Moss

EAN: 9781621137726
8 ½ x 10 ⅞, 32 pages
Product# 078010
$9.95 U.S., $11.95 Can.